Scripture quotations are from the NEW KING JAMES VERSION. Copyright © 1979, 1980, 1982, Thomas Nelson, Inc., Publishers.

Copyright © 1985 by Thomas Nelson Publishers.

Published in Nashville, Tennessee, by Thomas Nelson, Inc., and distributed in Canada by Lawson Falle, Ltd., Cambridge, Ontario.

First published in Great Britain by Creative Publishing, Northwood HA6 2HR, in 1985. Compiled and typeset by Creative Editors & Writers Ltd

International photographs in this series by R.F. Hicks, A, Bedding, D. Townsend, A. Hayward, S. Zisman, Frank Lane Agency (L. West)

You Can Be Full of Joy

— A Special Bible —

When the King James Version *of the Bible
was commissioned, few people would have guessed
that it would become the world's best seller,
year after year, decade after decade,
and century after century.
George Bernard Shaw, referring to its translators,
wrote of their 'boundless reverence and care'
and 'beautifully artistic result'.
The* New King James Version, *used in this book,
continues the labors of the earlier translators,
unlocking for today's readers the spiritual treasures
found in the* King James Version
of the Holy Scriptures.

— A Special Passage —

*You are almost certain to find
some of your favorite passages
in the following twenty pages of readings
from the* New King James Version *of the Bible.
The theme of joy will lift your spirits,
encourage you when you are discouraged,
and strengthen your resolve to
rejoice in the Lord every day.*

— A Famous Promise —

The Bible is shot through with promises,
promises from the Lord God himself
and from the Lord Jesus Christ.
These promises are meant to guide and comfort us
on our earthly pilgrimage.
The last three pages of this book
consist entirely of Bible promises
and short informal prayers
to strengthen our walk with God.

— A Famous Prayer —

People in every century of the Christian era
have prayed their own special prayers to God.
Using such prayers today
can inject a freshness into our own prayer life.
Augustine, Henry Martyn,
Nicholas Ridley, Charles Wesley,
Sadhu Sundar Singh,
Anselm, Johann Kepler
and F. M. Dostoevsky,
among others.

CONTENTS

JOY FROM THE FATHER

Paul wrote:

> Now may the God of hope
> fill you with all joy
> and peace in believing,
> that you may abound in hope
> by the power of the Holy Spirit.
> ROMANS 15:13

A parable from Jesus:

> 'What woman, having ten silver coins, if she loses
> one coin, does not light a lamp, sweep the house,
> and seek diligently until she finds it? And when she
> has found it, she calls her friends and neighbours
> together, saying, "Rejoice with me, for I have found
> the piece which I lost!" Likewise, I say to you,
> there is joy in the presence of the angels of God
> over one sinner who repents.'
> LUKE 15:8–10

A Famous Prayer

O God, You are Life, Wisdom, Truth,
Eternal, and the only true Good!
You are my God and Lord, my hope
and my heart's joy. Amen.
Anselm (1033–1109)

JOY IN GOD'S PRESENCE

The Psalmist wrote:

> You have made him exceedingly glad
> with your presence.
> PSALM 21:6

> I have set the LORD always before me;
> Because he is at my right hand
> I shall not be moved.
> Therefore my heart is glad,
> and my glory rejoices;
> My flesh also will rest in hope.
> … In your presence is fullness of joy;
> At your right hand
> are pleasures for evermore.
> PSALM 16:8–11

A Famous Prayer

*When thou art our strength
then we are strong,
but when we are our own strength
then we are weak.
Our good ever lives in thy presence.
O Lord, we return to thee now.
Lord, be ever with us.
Amen.*
St Patrick (389–461)

JOY FROM JESUS

Jesus promises

'These things I have spoken to you,
that my joy may remain in you,
and that your joy may be full.'
JOHN 15:11

Jesus prays to his Father

'Now I come to you,
and these things I speak in the world,
that they may have my joy
fulfilled in themselves.'
JOHN 17:13

A Famous Prayer

Dark and cheerless is the morn
Unaccompanied by thee;
Joyless is the day's return,
Till thy mercy's beams I see;
Till they inward light impart,
Glad my eyes, and warm my heart.
More and more thyself display,
Shining to the perfect day.
Amen.

Charles Wesley (1707–1788)

JOY FROM THE SPIRIT

Paul wrote:

The kingdom of God is not food and drink,
but righteousness and peace
and joy in the Holy Spirit.
ROMANS 14:17

And you became followers of us and of the Lord,
having received the word in much affliction,
with joy of the Holy Spirit.
1 THESSALONIANS 1:6

Jesus explains:

When he, the Spirit of truth, has come,
he will guide you into all truth.
JOHN 16:13

A Famous Prayer

*Heavenly Father, your wisdom is deep as
a fathomless sea; please send your Holy
Spirit into our hearts, and enlighten our
minds with the beams of your heavenly grace.
We ask this for our Savior's sake.
Amen.*

Nicholas Ridley (1500–1555)

Joy in Praising God

The Psalmist wrote:

But let all those rejoice
who put their trust in you;
Let them ever shout for joy,
because you defend them;
Let those also who love your name
Be joyful in you.
PSALM 5:11

The Psalmist praises God

Praise the LORD!
Praise, O servants of the LORD,
Praise the name of the LORD!
Blessed be the name of the LORD
From this time forth and for evermore!
PSALM 113:1–2

A Famous Prayer

When all thy mercies, O my God,
My rising soul surveys,
Transported with the view, I'm lost
In wonder, love, and praise.
Amen.
Joseph Addison (1672–1719)

JOY IN HEAVEN

A parable from Jesus

'What man of you, having a hundred sheep, if he loses one of them, does not leave the ninety-nine in the wilderness, and go after the one which is lost until he finds it? And when he has found it, he lays it on his shoulders, rejoicing. And when he comes home, he calls together his friends and neighbours, saying to them, "Rejoice with me, for I have found my sheep which was lost!"

I say to you that likewise there will be more joy in heaven over one sinner who repents than over ninety-nine just persons who need no repentance.'

LUKE 15:4–7

A Famous Prayer

Yea, amen, let all adore thee,
High on thine eternal throne;
Savior, take the power and glory:
Claim the kingdom as thine own:
Alleluia!
Thou shalt reign, and thou alone.
Amen.

Charles Wesley (1707–1788)

JOY OVERFLOWING

Paul wrote:

In a great trial of affliction
the abundance of their joy and their deep poverty
abounded in the riches of their liberality.
2 CORINTHIANS 8:2

Let love be without hypocrisy.
Abhor what is evil.
Cling to what is good.
Be kindly affectionate to one another with
brotherly love, in honour giving preference
to one another; not lagging behind in
diligence, fervent in spirit,
serving the Lord;
rejoicing in hope.
ROMANS 12:9–12

A Famous Prayer

*Dear Master, your many blessings and gifts
have filled my heart to overflowing
with gratitude and praise.
Thanks and praise be to thee
that I may rejoice in the fellowship
of your love.
Amen.*

Sadhu Sundar Singh (1889–1929?)

JOY WITHOUT MEASURE

Paul wrote:

I am filled with comfort.
I am exceedingly joyful in all our tribulation.
2 CORINTHIANS 7:4

Jesus taught:

'Blessed are you when men hate you,
And when they exclude you,
And revile you, and cast out your name as evil,
For the Son of Man's sake.
Rejoice in that day and leap for joy!
For indeed your reward is great in heaven,
For in like manner their fathers
did to the prophets.'
LUKE 6:22–23

A Famous Prayer

Lord, let me have no will of my own;
or consider my true happiness as
depending in the smallest degree
on anything that can befall me outwardly,
but as consisting altogether
in conformity with your will.
Amen.
Henry Martyn (1781–1812)

JOY WITHIN

The Psalmist wrote:

> You have put gladness in my heart,
> More than in the season
> that their grain and wine increased.
> PSALM 4:7

> Light is sown for the righteous,
> And gladness for the upright in heart.
> Rejoice in the LORD,
> you righteous,
> And give thanks
> at the remembrance of his holy name.
> PSALM 97:11–12

A Famous Prayer

Eternal God,
the light of the minds that know you,
the joy of the hearts that love you,
and the strength of the wills that serve you;
grant us so to know you
that we may truly love you,
and so to love you
that we may fully serve you,
whom to serve is perfect freedom,
in Jesus Christ our Lord. Amen.
Augustine (354–430)

JOY IN PRAYER

Paul wrote:

> Rejoice always,
> pray without ceasing,
> in everything give thanks;
> for this is the will of God
> in Christ Jesus for you.
>
> 1 THESSALONIANS 5:16–18

The Psalmist wrote:

> And my soul shall be joyful in the LORD;
> It shall rejoice in his salvation.
>
> PSALM 35:9

A Famous Prayer

Fill thou my life, O Lord my God,
In every part with praise,
That my whole being may proclaim
Thy being and thy ways.

Fill every part of me with praise:
Let all my being speak
Of thee and of thy love, O Lord,
Poor though I be and weak.
Amen.

H. Bonar (1808–1889)

JOY WHEN TRUSTING GOD

Oh, send out your light and your truth!
Let them lead me;
Let them bring me to your holy hill
And to your tabernacle.
Then I will go to the altar of God,
To God my exceeding joy;
And on the harp I will praise you,
O God, my God.

Why are you cast down, O my soul?
And why are you disquieted within me?
Hope in God;
For I shall yet praise him,
The help of my countenance
and my God.

PSALM 43:3–5

A Famous Prayer

Here, may my knowledge of you increase;
in heaven, may it be made perfect.
Here, may my love for you grow;
in heaven, may it be made perfect.
Then my joy in trusting you
will be made perfect.
Amen.

Anselm (1033–1109)

JOY THAT CAN NEVER BE TAKEN AWAY

Jesus told his disciples:

'Therefore you now have sorrow;
but I will see you again
and your heart will rejoice,
and your joy no one will take from you.'
JOHN 16:22

From the Book of Acts

[Paul and Silas were] beaten with rods.
And when they had laid many stripes on them,
they threw them into prison, commanding the jailer to
keep them securely.... But at midnight Paul and Silas
were praying and singing hymns to God,
and the prisoners were listening to them.
ACTS 16:22–25

A Famous Prayer

A safe stronghold our God is still,
A trusty shield and weapon;
He'll help us clear from all the ill
That hath us now o'ertaken.
Amen.
Martin Luther (1483–1546)
Translated by Thomas Carlyle

Joy that is Full

Jesus said:

'Whatever you ask the Father in my name
he will give you.
Until now you have asked nothing in my name.
Ask, and you will receive, that your joy
may be full.'
JOHN 16:23–24

From the Book of Acts

They departed ... rejoicing that they were
counted worthy to suffer shame for his name.
ACTS 5:41

A Famous Prayer

Our Savior, Lord Jesus.
Our hearts are cold;
Lord, warm them with your selfless love.
Our hearts are full of sin;
Lord, cleanse them with your blood.
Our hearts are feeble;
Lord, strengthen them with your Spirit.
Our hearts are empty;
Lord, fill them with your presence.
Amen.
Augustine (354–430)

Joy in Finding Jesus

Jesus said:

'The kingdom of heaven
is like treasure hidden in a field,
which a man found and hid;
and for joy over it he goes and sells
all that he has and buys that field.'
MATTHEW 13:44

The risen Jesus speaks to his disciples

'Peace be with you.'
… Then the disciples were glad
when they saw the Lord.
JOHN 20:19–20

A Famous Prayer

O let me see thy footmarks,
And in them plant mine own;
My hope to follow duly
Is in thy strength alone;
O guide me, call me, draw me,
Uphold me to the end;
And then in heaven receive me,
My Saviour and my Friend.
Amen.
J. E. Bode (1816–1874)

JOY IN NATURE

The Psalmist wrote:

> Let the heavens rejoice,
> and let the earth be glad;
> Let the sea roar,
> and all its fullness;
> Let the field be joyful,
> and all that is in it.
> Then all the trees of the woods
> will rejoice before the LORD.
> PSALM 96:11–12

> O LORD, our Lord,
> How excellent is your name
> in all the earth,
> You who set your glory above the heavens!
> PSALM 8:1

─A Famous Prayer─

*I thank you, my Creator and Lord, that
you have given me these joys in your
creation, this ecstasy over the work
of your hands. I have made known the
glory of your works to men as far as
my finite spirit was able to
comprehend your infinity.
Amen.*

Johann Kepler (1571–1630)

JOY IN THE WONDERS OF NATURE

The Psalmist wrote:

For you, LORD, have made me glad through your work;
I will triumph in the works of your hands.
PSALM 92:4

Praise the LORD!
Praise the LORD from the heavens;
Praise him in the heights!
Praise him, all his angels;
Praise him, all his hosts!
Praise him, sun and moon;
Praise him, all you stars of light!
Praise him, you heavens of heavens,
And you waters above the heavens!
PSALM 148:1–4

A Famous Prayer

Lord, may I love all thy creation,
the whole and every grain of sand in it.
May I love every leaf,
every ray of this light.
May I love the animals.
Amen.
F. M. Dostoevsky (1821–1881)

JOY AT JESUS' BIRTH

Luke wrote:

Then the angel said to them,
'Do not be afraid, for behold, I bring you
good tidings of great joy which will be to
all people. For there is born to you this day
in the city of David a Savior, who is Christ
the Lord. And this will be the sign to you:
You will find a babe wrapped in
swaddling cloths, lying in a manger.'
And suddenly there was with the angel
a multitude of the heavenly host
praising God and saying:
   'Glory to God in the highest,
     And on earth peace, good will towards men!'
LUKE 2:10—14

A Famous Prayer

Angels, from the realms of glory,
Wing your flight o'er all the earth;
Ye who sang creation's story
Now proclaim Messiah's birth:
   Come and worship,
    Worship Christ, the new-born King. Amen.

J. Montgomery (1771–1854)

JOY AT JESUS' RESURRECTION

Matthew wrote:

[The angel said,]
'Go quickly
and tell his disciples
that he is risen from the dead,
and indeed he is going before you
into Galilee;
there you will see him.
Behold, I have told you.'
So they departed quickly from the tomb
with fear
and great joy,
and ran to bring his disciples word.
MATTHEW 28:7–8

A Famous Prayer

Jesus Christ is risen to-day,
    Alleluia!
Our triumphant holy day,
    Alleluia!
Who did once, upon the cross,
    Alleluia!
Suffer to redeem our loss.
Alleluia!
Amen
Anon, from 'Lyra Davidica' (1708)

JOY IN WORSHIPING GOD

The Psalmist wrote:

> Oh come, let us sing to the LORD!
> Let us shout joyfully
> to the Rock of our salvation.
> PSALM 95:1

Luke wrote:

> They worshipped him, and returned to Jerusalem
> with great joy, and were continually in the
> temple, praising and blessing God. Amen.
> LUKE 24:52–53

Isaiah the prophet wrote:

> Sing to the LORD,
> For he has done excellent things;
> This is known in all the earth.
> ISAIAH 12:5

A Famous Prayer

*Thou madest me for thyself,
and my heart is restless
until it rests in thee.
Amen.*
Augustine (354–430)

JOY IN SERVING JESUS

Luke wrote:

Then the seventy returned with joy, saying,
'Lord, even the demons
are subject to us in your name.'
And he said to them,
'I saw Satan fall like lightning from heaven.
Behold, I give you the authority
to trample on serpents and scorpions,
and over all the power of the enemy,
and nothing shall by any means hurt you.
Nevertheless do not rejoice in this,
that the spirits are subject to you,
but rejoice rather
because your names are written in heaven.'
LUKE 10:17–20

—A Famous Prayer—

My Savior,
take my mouth,
to spread abroad the glory of thy name.
Take all my powers,
for the advancement of thy people.
Never allow the steadfastness
and confidence of my faith to abate.
Amen.

D. L. Moody (1837–1899)

A Word of Comfort

and Prayer for ...

◆ **When I feel joyless**
John 15:11 Jesus promises 'These things I have
spoken to you, that my joy may remain in you, and
that your joy may be full.'
Prayer: *Dear Lord, fill my life with your presence
today, so that I may know your joy in my life. Amen.*

◆ **When I am laughed at for being a
Christian**
Luke 6:22–23 'Blessed are you when men hate you, and
when they exclude you, and revile you, and cast out
your name as evil, for the Son of Man's sake. Rejoice in
that day and leap for joy! For indeed your reward is
great in heaven, for in like manner their fathers did to
the prophets.'
Prayer: *Lord Jesus, you went through so much more
persecution than I ever will. May I bring credit to you
when I suffer for you. Amen.*

◆ **When I feel like praising God**
Psalm 35:9 'My soul shall be joyful in the LORD; it shall
rejoice in his salvation.'
Prayer: *Dear Lord, I pour out my heart in praise and
thanks to you today for your goodness to me. Amen.*

◆ When I am sad

John 16:22 Jesus said: 'Therefore you now have sorrow; but I will see you again and your heart will rejoice, and your joy no one will take from you.'

Prayer: Dear Lord Jesus, you never said that your followers would be free from sadness. So in my sadness help me to rely on you and on the deep joy you give, which nobody can take away and nothing can destroy. Amen.

◆ When I don't feel like praying

John 16:23 'Whatever you ask the Father in my name he will give you.'

Prayer: Lord Jesus, thank you that I belong to you because you died for me. Help me to come to you in prayer every day. Amen.

◆ When I am rejoicing in God's salvation

Matthew 13:44 'The kingdom of heaven is like treasure hidden in a field.'

Prayer: Lord Jesus, I did indeed find treasure when you revealed your love to me. Thank you for making me your own. Amen.

◆ When I have doubts about my Christian faith

John 20:19–20 'Jesus said: "Peace be with you."… Then the disciples were glad when they saw the Lord.'

Prayer: Lord Jesus, the important thing is to have faith in you and not in myself or anything else. Please strengthen me to keep looking to you. Amen.

◆ **When I want the world to know about Jesus**

Psalm 8:1 'O LORD, our Lord, how excellent is your name in all the earth, you who set your glory above the heavens!'

Prayer: Dear Lord, you are the great God and everything belongs to you. Help me to tell others about you. Let my whole life sing your praises. Amen.

◆ **When I want the whole of my being to praise God!**

Psalm 148:1 'Praise the LORD! Praise the LORD from the heavens; praise him in the heights!'

Prayer: Heavenly Father, I worship you and praise you today. You are the creator and sustainer of the world. How I long for everyone and everything to praise your name! Amen.

◆ **When I forget that Jesus is the centre of our lives**

Luke 2:10–11 'Then the angel said to them, "Do not be afraid, for behold, I bring you good tidings of great joy which will be to all people. For there is born to you this day in the city of David a Savior, who is Christ the Lord."'

Prayer: Dear Lord Jesus, you came into our world to bring the good news of salvation. All those who receive you into their lives must acknowledge you as Lord. Help me to put you first in my life. Amen.